EMERGE POSITIVE

Daily Affirmations to Uplift and Inspire

Deanne Lewis

Balboa Press books may be ordered through booksellers or by contacting:

Balboa Press
A Division of Hay House
1663 Liberty Drive
Bloomington, IN 47403
www.balboapress.com
1 (877) 407-4847

Because of the dynamic nature of the Internet, any web addresses or links contained in this book may have changed since publication and may no longer be valid. The views expressed in this work are solely those of the author and do not necessarily reflect the views of the publisher, and the publisher hereby disclaims any responsibility for them.

Any people depicted in stock imagery provided by Thinkstock are models, and such images are being used for illustrative purposes only. Certain stock imagery © Thinkstock.

Cover photo by Asha Guenther

ISBN: 978-1-4525-9902-1 (sc)
ISBN: 978-1-4525-9901-4 (e)

Library of Congress Control Number: 2014920787

Printed in the United States of America.

Balboa Press rev. date: 01/15/2015

BALBOA
PRESS
A DIVISION OF HAY HOUSE

To Lon,
who has taught me that with love, hope and enthusiasm;
anything is possible.

Emerge (verb.)

/e-merg/

1. to come forth into view or notice, as from concealment or obscurity

2. to rise or come forth

3. become known

4. to come into existence; develop.

5. to be revealed

Positive (adj., noun.)

/pos-i-tiv/

1. Showing optimism and confidence

2. A good, affirmative, or constructive quality or attribute

3. Constructive in intention or attitude

4. Showing pleasing progress, gain or improvement

5. With no possibility of doubt; clear and definite

EMERGE POSITIVE

The commitment to find, reveal and love your true
self, and to live each day with confidence knowing
all is well.

Life isn't handed to you – it's a creation; a dance with God – and it's as big as you believe it to be.

Emerge Positive

When you love who you are, life immediately is better

A good life begins when you love who you are. If you don't love yourself, how can you expect others to love you? You will give what you have inside to give. When you are filled with love and happiness, that is what comes through to others. So, step one in changing your life is to love yourself. That means your extra weight, your nose, your greying hair....all of it. And as you begin to embrace you, the things you didn't like before will change; because your perception will change. So start here: Be you, give to others and love in abundance. Emerge Positive

Lack only exists
if you believe
in it

Whenever I catch myself feeling like I'm lacking something in my life, I go outside and look around. It's a great reminder of the beautiful abundance all around us. Instead of thinking about what you don't have, focus on what you do. For where you put your focus and energy, it will grow. Get rid of the lack in your life by focusing on the simple abundance that exists all around us. Emerge Positive

Your words and actions are powerful to those around you. Today, take notice of the impact of your actions. Not only to people, but to our world. For us to survive as a whole, we need to live consciously -- aware of every choice we make. Because what you do matters. Good choices will help others and cultivate a beautiful Earth. Be aware today and Emerge Positive.

Be aware of the
impact of your
actions

A cluttered home

creates

a cluttered mind

Take 30 minutes out of your weekend to clear your space. If that seems overwhelming, pick one thing: a countertop that seems to collect things, a junk drawer, your desk....whatever is most visibly cluttered in your home. Clearing the space opens the energy flow. And that will positively impact your spirit... it will clear your mind and lift your mood. It's simple, easy and worth every minute. Enjoy your day! Emerge Positive

From time to time, it is normal to reflect on your life. Reflection is important, but don't get bogged down in the trials and disappointments...instead, focus on where you are going. Look forward and see the life you will create. See it, feel it and know it is there waiting for you. *Emerge Positive*

No need to look back, you've already been there . . . focus forward and fly

Stop wishing and start doing

Today is a new opportunity to create the life you want. Do you know what that is? To lose weight? Be healthy? To start a new career? Whatever it is, you have an opportunity to do something about it today. Sitting around wishing it to be won't help you....you must take action. What are you waiting for? Pick one thing that will start the momentum. Just one step is all it takes. *Emerge Positive*

Sometimes what we think we want isn't what is best for us. Trust life will bring you to your purpose.

S ometimes what we want isn't meant for us. And the only way to know for sure is to let go. Step back and give some space between you and the idea. We are all here for a purpose and that can only unfold if you let it. If you are completely focused on something else, you'll miss it. So if something isn't working out the way you hoped, don't worry. It's just life pushing you in the direction you need to go. Emerge Positive

Simplify your life

Material goods do not fill the void inside. They may feel good for the initial purchase, but after a period of time that high will wear off and you'll be off to the next purchase in search for peace and wholeness. Nothing outside of yourself will bring you peace. That can only come from within. Enjoy the abundance of this world! But don't look to it for your happiness...if you do, you will be continuously disappointed. Slow down today and enjoy the simple things in life. Take note of all the beauty and love that is within you and surrounding you right now. Yes, life is abundant indeed. Emerge Positive

Love Yourself

No matter what the problem, the main issue to work on is loving yourself. *Emerge Positive*

Life is busy and often we run so hard, we forget to say Thanks. Today, take a moment to be grateful for life. To say thank you for your health, your relationships, the ability to see, smell, taste and touch. Life is abundant and beautiful. Say Thanks. *Emerge Positive*

Don't forget to say Thanks

*A*ny day is a perfect day to 'think fun'. Do something that will make you smile. Put down whatever burden you've been carrying around all week and breathe. Enjoy an ice cream cone, take a bubble bath, go for a walk, take 15 minutes to yourself, savor a piece of chocolate, share a good bottle of wine. Whatever you choose, enjoy every moment of it! Actually take the time to be in the moment of fun. Life doesn't have to be so serious... lighten up, smile, enjoy the fun and Emerge Positive.

Think fun

Put down the mobile device and give your full attention to someone who needs it

*E*verywhere I look, I see people buried in their phones and tablets. Calling someone is becoming a thing of the past. Text, messenger and email are the main forms of communication. And the ironic outcome of that is disconnection....with others, with the heart and with the whole. Today, dedicate some time to unplug from your devices. And instead, spend some quality time with someone who needs it....you may find that the person is you. Emerge Positive

Dreams are
realized one step
at a time.
Today, you just need
to take a step.

L ife can feel overwhelming at times -- so much to do and
not enough time to do it. How do we fit in the time needed
to pursue our dreams and happiness in the middle of the
chaos? By taking one step. That's it. One. And you can do that.
Each day, we just need to focus on that day - not tomorrow's class
or the deadline next week, just today. That's doable. So say it with
me, 'My dreams are being created right now with this one step'.
Emerge Positive

Fear is just a thought.
Don't let it
hold you back
from your dreams.

_____

We all give fear too much power. And it has stopped many of us from living our best life. Don't give in to fear. It is just a thought in your mind...that's it. Change the thought and move forward. It may not be as easy as it sounds, but you can do it! You can do anything you want if you believe it. So say it with me, "I will not let fear stand in my way today. I will begin living the life I desire." Go out there and love life. Be grateful for everything you have and go for it! Emerge Positive

_____

Healing begins
with a
willingness to let go.

We are all dealing with hurts...whether it be loneliness, financial struggles or health challenges...each of them causes us pain. As I sit with friends and strangers, I see the struggles all around. This world is in a dire need of healing. The first step is you...for once You heal, you demonstrate and give others the space to heal as well. Healing begins with self love and the willingness to let the pain go. Stop focusing on what is wrong and focus on what is good. Don't let anything get in your way of positive thought and healing. For what you believe will be. Today, take a stance that you will let go of the pain; let go of the idea of what you don't have and focus on the good. Healing begins with you. Emerge Positive

If you don't take care of yourself, who will? Healthy living is not difficult; it is a series of conscious choices. Start with the basics: a good night sleep (I like 7 hours), eat clean, organic food (lots of vegetables & fruit) in small servings, drink lots of water (8 glasses minimum), exercise daily doing an activity you enjoy and take some down time to relax each day. With these 5 simple things, you can turn your low energy day into a healthy, high energy and positive life. Remember, the choices you make now create your tomorrow....Emerge Positive.

Make healthy living a priority

What is your relationship to money? Do you see it as bad? Something you will never have? Something you can't have? If you hold any negative thoughts about money in your mind, you will not experience material abundance. Money isn't bad. It's a form of trade...that's it. Change your thoughts about money and you will change the flow of it in your life. Start to see money as a river...one that flows through you and is never ending. As it passes through, you have the opportunity to use it for good. To bless it along the way and send it back into the world with a new positive healing energy. Everything in this world can be used for good....including money. Today, pay attention to your beliefs and thoughts about money. If they aren't positive, start to change them and watch your life begin to change as well. Emerge Positive

Money is not the problem; it's our relationship to it that is

You are not your past
Forgive and
move forward

We tend to hang onto disappointments and hurts in our heart. And that can be very dangerous and hurtful to ourselves. Anger, sadness and fear held within turn into disease in our body. Don't do it. The only person that suffers is you. I know you may be angry about your childhood, your parents, the unfair life that you experienced, but let it go. It is not your life now....unless you choose to carry it with you. If you truly want to be free and begin anew, let go. Just put it down and walk forward. Emerge Positive

The sixth sense, the voice within, 'gut check' Listen to it

We all have intuition...some of us rely on it more than others. But it's there for us all. Whatever you call it....a gut feeling, a sixth sense or the voice within; listen to it. It's there to guide you and help. Don't brush it aside, no matter how crazy it may seem. Personally, my life works better when I'm listening and acting on that guidance. Give it a try...we're not meant to figure it all out on our own. Rely on your internal guidance. Emerge Positive

Don't waste your time and energy on trivial things. Focus on what really matters in your life. Start taking care of yourself. Take some time for you. Breathe. Spend time with your family and friends. Stop obsessing about the extra 5 pounds around your waist or the balance in your checking account. If today were your last, would those things matter? Today is a gift -- take it all in and Emerge Positive.

Put your focus & energy on the things that matter

Nobody is better at being You than you are

You have a purpose in this life. Do you know what it is? Have you spent any time thinking about it? You bring something unique to this world that is meant to be shared. You are the best at being You and nobody is better at it than you. Don't try to be something else and stop listening to anyone that is trying to tell you otherwise. Just be you. *Emerge Positive*

The healthier you are in mind, body and spirit, the more beautiful you become. Remind yourself you are a work in progress and embrace the true beauty within. *Emerge Positive*

True beauty is the radiance that flows through someone who knows exactly who they are

Want a different
outcome?
Choose a different
perception

The fastest way to improve your life is to change your perception of it. Your thoughts create the life you live. This cannot be stressed enough. Pay attention to what you think. And if your thoughts are negative, purposefully push them out. You don't need negativity in your life....so don't allow those thoughts to seep in. Instead, choose to focus on the positive -- on the good in your life and the love that is in you and surrounding you. With a positive perception, you will see a change in everything and everyone around you! Emerge Positive

If you are looking for Love, Give Love and it will find you

This is a universal law.... you must Give to Receive. If you are worried about money, give to others. (this includes time, not just cash) If you are lonely, go spend time with someone who needs a friend. Giving comes in all forms. Life isn't all about you.... it's about how you choose to live and treat others. Love deeply and love all. Emerge Positive

It's good to have a plan and know the direction you want to go. But don't hold tightly to the outcome you want. Because often the very best things in life happen outside of your plan. Things you would have never dreamed of....bigger, better, miraculous things. When you agree to trust in the process, have faith in something bigger than yourself and just let go is when life will provide you the miracles you dream of. Emerge Positive

What happens outside of our plan is the good stuff

Once you
realize You are the root
cause of all your stress
is when change occurs

T his is a hard one to embrace, but it is truth. We choose how we react to each thing that crosses our path. No one can make us angry, or stressed or sad...that's our choice. And once you understand this, you will see that stress can go away as quickly as changing your thought. We are not victims...life doesn't happen to us; we aren't dealt a good hand or bad. Life is what you create it to be. It is what you believe it to be. Today, be open to the idea that you can have a different perception. And that what is stressing you out doesn't have to. Emerge Positive

I was up half the night with worrying thoughts that just wouldn't let me be. And now, in the daylight, all of those "nighttime worries" seem just silly. Why do we worry? It doesn't help the situation, us or the person/people we are worrying about! It just steals our energy, sleep and peace. Instead, we should stop ourselves right in the middle of the worrying thought and say, all is well, all will be well and all is well! I'm pushing worrying aside and moving forward in peace. Won't you join me? Emerge Positive

Worrying is a complete waste of your energy

When in doubt, give

Giving doesn't have to be money....but that is good to share too. For what you give, you receive. Today, be aware of your attitude towards giving. Are you coming to the table with a 'what's in it for me' or 'what can I give' attitude? Give a smile, a hug, an encouraging word, or buy someone a coffee. It doesn't take much effort to share love. And we all could use a little help and inspiration....so give today. Give with all your heart. Emerge Positive

I am a work

in progress

Perfection is something many strive for but at what cost? Embrace who you are right now. Love yourself and know you are here to experience life, learn and grow. We are all works in progress. Emerge Positive

Don't make the mistake of thinking you need (fill in the blank) before you can be happy. Life is happening now. Don't miss it waiting around for something else. The new car, the relationship, the promotion.... all good things, but don't put your happiness on hold while you wait. Enjoy your life right where you are. Emerge Positive

Enjoy life
right where
you are

Want to be a positive change
in the world?
Start with being who you
are, where you are, doing
what you do

Change starts with one person. You don't need to do something remarkable, life-changing or miraculous. Just be who you are....loving, caring, giving, helpful and empathetic. Be it every day in every situation. Don't let other people's actions or words distract you from who you are. Don't give them the power. Stay the course. You will be amazed at how many people watch what you do and how you do it. Your positive and loving attitude will make a difference. Be the change you want to see in the world...today. Emerge Positive

You have the power
to change the
outcome

Once you recognize you have the power to change the outcome, your life will automatically improve. Doing the same thing over and over while expecting a different result, is the definition of insanity. If you don't like the outcome, then step back and look at the situation differently. Consciously choose to shift your perception. And then go at it again. Life is what you perceive it to be. So don't make it depressing. Don't be a victim. You have the power to change...stand up and use it. Emerge Positive

Action is the way
through fear
Have faith and take
that step

Is there something you dream of doing? What's stopping you? Doubt and fear likely top the list. We all deal with fear in life. I've learned that fear doesn't go away, but you can walk through it. And when you do, it's powerful. You can do anything. You just have to believe you can. And once you hold that belief, Action is the key. Don't delay another day. Take a step forward - walk through the fear and Emerge Positive.

Demonstrate your faith

This could equally say, 'demonstrate your love'....for it is the same. Come to each situation, communication and experience with a purpose of being loving and helpful. Not with the attitude of "what's in it for me?" We are here to share, love and learn. And when we give, we expand whatever goodness is shared. If you want to make the world better, start right now with how you treat others. Come to the table with a helpful and loving heart and watch what happens. *Emerge Positive*

Have you ever hung on to anger? Or sat in frustration? I think we have all experienced those times when we just don't let it go. We hang onto the anger like a dog with a bone. And when we do that, it doesn't fix the situation and it actually is creating illness in our bodies. A healthy body and life begins with a positive mind. Let go of the anger, jealousy, frustration, negativity and *Emerge Positive*.

A positive mind creates a healthy body

*I*t's not about you....it never was. Our society tells us the opposite and supports the idea of a "me culture" everywhere we turn. The truth, however, is it's about the bigger picture. There is a larger presence/ creator running the show. Call it God, Universe, Energy, Divine.....whatever you choose, make that your focus. That in turn, will lead you down your chosen path with the goal of how you can serve the whole. And when that is your thought, everything good in life will begin to unfold. Emerge Positive

Put your focus on God and the rest will fall into place

Perception through eyes of Gratitude produces a blessed life

*B*egin your day by thinking of 5 things you are grateful for in your life. Just that simple step can change the course of your day. And if you do that daily, it will change the course of your life. Gratitude opens the heart and gives us new eyes. And how we see the world will create our beliefs and our actions. Imagine what our world would be like if gratitude were a focus? It starts with one.....Emerge Positive.

To your heart, your thoughts, to other people, to sounds of nature. Want to be better? Start listening more. *Emerge Positive*

Spend more time Listening

Slow down and be present

There is always so much going on, it is easy to be focused elsewhere and miss what is happening right in front of you. Today, make a conscious effort to slow down. Know that there is enough time in the day to get everything done. Life is not a sprint to the finish line. So why are you running? Stop and enjoy today. It is a gift and it holds so many little treasures that could otherwise go unfound. *Emerge Positive*

What you believe of yourself is what you are

Pay attention to your inner thoughts. When you see your reflection, what goes through your head? My nose is too big? I'm fat? This shirt looks awful on me? Stop the negative tape in your head....stop it as soon as you notice it. For your beliefs will become your truth. Practice this statement: "I am ___". Fill the blank with something positive about you and keep saying it over and over. For what you believe about yourself is true. I believe in you...it's time for you to start believing too. Emerge Positive

Take the time to tell the people in your life how grateful you are for them

Having a grateful heart is essential, but don't keep it all inside of you....share it with others. Words are powerful - it will create a wave that has a snowball effect to those around you. Tell at least one person in your life how grateful you are for their love, friendship, help, mentorship, etc. Create a wave of gratitude today and watch it grow. Emerge Positive

You are worth the wait.... Love yourself. Emerge Positive

Don't settle. Choose to be with someone that supports the authentic you.

Happiness is our own responsibility

Happiness doesn't just show up....you must choose it. It is a daily, moment to moment choice that comes from within. Your car, boyfriend, house or job won't bring it into your life. Oh, it might feel like it for a day or so, but external things don't create the joy you crave. So stop looking outside of yourself to be happy. Choose it today. Choose it now! You have limited time on this planet, so why wait one more minute? Take responsibility for your life and choose happiness. *Emerge Positive*

Get excited for the possibilities

I'm reminded this morning that the Universe is operating in harmony and that everything is happening in order. Often it looks dysfunctional and chaotic, and as a result, we fight against it. Today, try something new: let go, step back and get excited about the possibilities in your life. There is so much to look forward to....so much goodness and abundance available to you. Life is good. And your life doesn't have to be an exception to that. Open your mind to the idea that you have much to be excited about. Emerge Positive

Embrace

your own

You

Knowing and loving who you are is the key to a happy life. If you do nothing else, invest the time in you. *Emerge Positive*

You will experience an immense peace and freedom when you fully embrace this truth: You are enough. Right now. You don't need to lose weight, have a better hair style, wear trendy clothes or live in a better house. You don't need to do anything... love who you are and the rest will flow naturally. Peace, abundance and freedom occur when you are true to you. *Emerge Positive*

Who you are is enough

Have faith
There is a plan
and it stars you

Don't let yourself get comfortable and settle. There is a purpose and journey laid out specifically for you...don't stop short of it. Don't give up on your dreams and the excitement of what drives you. Believe there is a plan and you are exactly where you are meant to be right now. It might be difficult and challenging, but it's taking you to where you are meant to go next. Have faith. Know that your future is bright and keep moving forward. After all, this is your experience...so live it! Emerge Positive

You already have everything you need

Whatever it is that you want to do, know you have everything you need right now to start it. Often, we think we need to be better, more knowledgable, in better shape, etc to start our project or goals. But the fact is, you wouldn't have the desire to start this project if it weren't meant for you! We all have purpose in this world and frankly, we need each other to bring to life those projects that are meant for us. Don't delay...don't make others wait that need to experience your gifts. Take that first step. *Emerge Positive*

---

*A great day starts
with a good
night's sleep*

Many of us overlook the importance of sleep. It is one of the essential pieces to healthy living....right up there with diet and exercise. So why are we so quick to ignore it? The body needs rest to rejuvenate itself for the next day. Without that, your energy level suffers, which causes brain fogginess, which can lead to poor choices made in your day. Make the decision that your health is important! And tonight, allow yourself the time for sleep. It's the perfect set up for a great day. *Emerge Positive*

Don't be afraid of the unknown. For what is known is our past. The unknown is our future. Embrace the adventure and expect miracles. Holding onto fear will only get in the way and make your experience small. And life is anything but small. Let go... control is an illusion. When you fully embrace that, you will be able to enjoy each moment as it unfolds. Emerge Positive

Expect miracles

Stop limiting God

Anything is possible, if you believe in it. When we forget this, is when doubt and worry set in. And these are the two blocks that we all let into our lives. They are the ropes that hold us back. Whatever it is that you dream of, allow yourself to believe it's possible. Because with God, anything is possible. Don't create obstacles....believe there is a path for you and take it. Emerge Positive

There are two paths:
Fear or Love.
It's your choice

You have a choice in how you live your life. Are you choosing Love or Fear? It seems like a ridiculous question, but many of us choose fear. All of our stresses, anger, frustration and negativity come from the path of fear. So when you catch yourself over there, stop and change direction. Remind yourself today that it is your choice...people can't make you angry. That's your chosen reaction. And you can change that in any given moment. Don't let others dictate your day. Choose Love. Emerge Positive

Life is so busy, it's easy to let 'friend time' slip. But time with true friends is unlike anything else. Those people who really know you, who accept you and let you Be You .... well, those relationships are gifts. We get energized just being around them. Joy, happiness and love are so present that we can actually feel giddy. Don't put off seeing a good friend. It may seem like a trivial thing, but it's not - it's a necessity. It's a gift to embrace. A true friend is medicine for the Soul. Emerge Positive

Time spent with true friends is medicine for the soul

Never miss a chance to Dance

When I was younger, I worried too much about what others thought of me. And as a result, I missed out on many chances to Dance in life. Have you done that too? Now looking back, it seems downright silly. Make the decision to dance in life. Don't miss it and definitely don't pass it up when it is presented to you in your day. Dance off the stress, dance to bring a smile, dance to share fun with others.....Life is filled with opportunities to Dance. Don't miss them. Emerge Positive

Laughter has healing powers. No matter your mood or circumstance, a good laugh can lift your spirits high. Laughter shared between friends or family is good for the soul. So today, lighten up and laugh. Not only will you feel better, you'll also be reminded that life doesn't have to be so serious. Emerge Positive

Let Laughter lift you up

Change the way you think and you will change your life

Our thoughts are what creates our day and therefore, our life. Pay attention to what you are thinking about....is it negative? Are you saying you need to lose weight? That you're not good enough? That you're lonely? Then that is exactly what will come to be.....change your thoughts. What you think about comes about. Thoughts are energy and they will shape your future. So you choose...negative or positive? Emerge Positive

It's a new day! A new opportunity to begin again, try something new, stretch yourself and enjoy. Why waste this precious day in a bad mood? Don't let other people's actions or words change your course. This is your day! And it's a gift. Be grateful and embrace each moment. Emerge Positive

If you woke up today, you already have something to be Grateful for

Spread Love

We are here to love. Bring love into everything you do....including your job. What you do each day isn't important, it's How you do it. When you bring love into every word and action in your day, it heals. Love is contagious. It can't be missed by others. They may not be able to put their finger on it, but they will notice. And you will be making a difference. Make the choice to spread love today. Emerge Positive

Dare to be You

Believe in yourself. Stop thinking that you need to be something else to be accepted and loved by others. You don't. You were made for a purpose. Embrace it. Be it! Dare to be You. Emerge Positive

---

You are already perfect and whole. There is no need to gain approval from anyone else. Do your job, your task, your errands to your best ability. Don't do them in order to get someone's attention or approval. That's not being true to yourself. Don't let others define who you are....that only comes from within. So don't be fooled. Live life as You....period. Emerge Positive

When you look to the world for approval, you will always be disappointed

We must believe
it before we can
see it

One of the most important things you can do for yourself is to learn how to control your mind. For what you think about, comes about. Everything that is around you, first began as a thought or idea. What you want to have or experience in your life is no different. Focus your thoughts on the positive things, on your dreams, on the life you wish to live. Push out the fear, doubt and worry....they aren't real; they are just thoughts that will be created unless you push them aside. You have the power to create....use it wisely and Emerge Positive.

Who says you have to do something 'their way'? Why not break off and start your own path? This is your life, your time, your adventure....why follow others? Show off your unique, creative self! Be you! Because you aren't just a number in the room.... you are here for a purpose. So, stop following the herd and start creating the life you want. That can start right now. Dare to be different. Emerge Positive

Make your own path

You create your future by choices made today. And that future is bright when your choices are based on the truth of who you are

Know who you are....seems like an odd statement, but it is essential. Otherwise, you will live a life trying to be what you think others expect and that's just a waste of the authentic you! Be true to yourself and bring your heart and talent into everything you do -- the result... more joy and happiness for you and everyone around you. Emerge Positive

Honor yourself in all you do

When you know and like who you are, it's pretty easy to honor that person in every situation. But if you aren't connected with the real you, it's not that easy. When going through your day, be aware of how you are presenting yourself - the words you are using - your actions. Do they honor you? Are you being true to who you are, what you stand for and represent? Don't let yourself think that you need to be something better. You don't need to wear a mask today. You don't need to cover up. Honor the wonderful person you are and Emerge Positive.

You bring people, things and situations into your life that match your beliefs. It's magnetic. Therefore, it's essential to know your worth...to believe the value you have in this world. And don't allow anything less in your life. Know it, believe it and be it. Emerge Positive

Know your worth and don't accept anything less

Don't give up.
When opposition
is at its peak
is when your victory
is closest

We give up too easily. Opposition isn't a bad thing...it shows you how much you want something. If you turn now, you just may be walking away from the thing you want most. You never know how many doors you will walk through to reach your goal, but know it is there waiting for you. Don't give up. Keep going...and know that belief, persistence and determination will bring you there. Emerge Positive

Don't overlook the climb up. It's the most important part.

We often are so focused on reaching the goal, that we completely miss the journey. And the journey is the most important part. Life isn't about standing on top of the mountain....it's about the climb up. So if you are in the middle of your climb, stop for a moment and look around. Take it in. Enjoy it. This is life happening right now. Don't miss it. Emerge Positive

Failure is part of success. For many of us, this roots us in fear, unable to try what we desire. However, fear is just a thought...it's not real. And the reality is, we all learn best by failing. So if you are stuck, take a step forward and try. If you've already taken the step and fallen, congratulations! You're one step closer to success! Get up, try again and fail better. Emerge Positive

Keep going. Fail better

The easiest way to improve your life is to change your thinking. Whenever you notice a negative thought, push it aside. You may be surprised to notice all the negative thoughts we let in. Don't beat yourself up about it, just move on to the next positive thought. Our thoughts create our reality...our life. So pay attention to your thinking; it will create a result that is worth the effort. Emerge Positive

Positive thinking creates positive change -- in your words, actions and life

Sometimes we have to get out of our own way

Sometimes we are our own worst enemy. Our negative self talk and thoughts literally stop us from what we want. We get in our own way! The good news is, you have all the power to change that. Begin to speak positive thoughts and state your purpose in the present tense (not future), then step aside. When you do, you will create an opening to take a step forward and Emerge Positive.

Today is a new

opportunity to

create the life

you want

I'm grateful for a new day. It's like a do-over button is available to us every 24 hours. How will you spend your time today? How will it benefit you? How will it help others? If you are looking for change or improvement in your life, do something today that will take you one step closer to what you want. Just one step. All we have is today....tomorrow isn't here yet. So make the most of it. Have fun, be joyful and Emerge Positive.

Choose Happiness

A new day..... It's time for an improved outlook and attitude. Today, remind yourself that your day will be exactly as you choose. It's not up to anyone else. So make the choice to be happy! Choose to see the glass half full. Create a day that is fun! And spread the joy. This world desperately needs it. So give it out in large doses today and Emerge Positive.

Printed in the United States
By Bookmasters